The Journey of Life

I'm Better Because of It

SAMUEL MCGILL III, Th.B.

© 2016 The Journey of Life-I'm Better Because of It
All Rights Reserved.

No part of this book may be reproduced, stored in a retrieval system, or transmitted by any means without the written permission of the author.

Published by Word Therapy Publishing
November 14, 2016

ISBN-13: 978-0975516317

ISBN-10: 0975516310

Printed in the United States of America all rights reserved under international Copyright laws. The views expressed in this work are solely those of the author and do not necessarily reflect the views of the publisher, and the publisher hereby disclaims any responsibility for them

Cover Design by: SharperFX, Atlanta, GA

word therapy
PUBLISHING

Word Therapy Publishing
P.O. Box 939
Hope Mills, NC 28348
www.wordtherapypublishing.com
888-494-8880

Dedication

This book is dedicated to
Derrick Trevon Watts-McGill
(My Deceased Son)

When I thought about whom I would dedicate this book to three people immediately come to mind besides God. Those three people are Augustine McGill, Mattie C. Simmons and Martha Thirkield. My mother, my grandmother and my aunt. There would not be a Bishop Samuel McGill III without the contribution that these women made in my life. Each had their role and responsibility but the sum total of who I am is because of what each gave to me. I will forever love each of them. May they rest in peace.

Acknowledgements

~RIDE THE WAVE~

First I must give honor to God for without him I can do nothing.

To Alexus S. McGill and Adaysha M. McGill my two daughters who absolutely have been a source of strength in my life and have helped me to be able to make it on this journey called "Life."

To Tonja, Riley and Portia I love you guys with all my heart. Thanks for reminding me that magic still happens!

To the Honorable Bishop Charles H. Ellis, III and the AGAPE Fellowship of Pastors.

To Bishop Willie Martin, Jr., Elder Benjamin Akins, Elder Ivan Elam and Ronnie Timmons who are true friends and men of God that I love and respect very highly. Thanks for being the fulfillment of scripture, "A Friend Loves at All Times!!"

To Dr. Pauline Key a true lifetime friend!

To Toni Henderson-Mayers and the entire staff of Word Therapy Publishing who pushed me to get this body of work out. I appreciate you all so much.

To my brother Mario McGill I am proud of you man. Always remember this, "At the end of the day, You're a Man of God!!"

To the All Nations Riders who are truly ride or die. You all are some of the most amazing people. Thanks for allowing me to encourage you and speak into your lives. You guys ROCK!!!

Table of Contents

Chapter 1: Growing up in a Hard Environment

Chapter 2: Dealing with the Loss of My Father

Chapter 3: Dealing with the Loss of My Son

Chapter 4: The Brig

Chapter 5: Wounded in the Church

Chapter 6: Burying My Mother

Chapter 7: Time and Chance (Hotel Experience)

Chapter 8: Even the Leaders Hurt

Chapter 9: Suffering for The Glory

Chapter 10: Healing and Restoration

Chapter 11: I'm Better Because of It

Chapter One

Growing Up in A Hard Environment

Mobile, Alabama becomes now the canvas by which I begin to paint the picture of my journey. Life has a funny way of throwing things at you. I grew up in an area that was called "The Campground." I can't remember our house number but it was on Basil Street and I also have a very faint recollection of things growing up there in terms of family activity but I do remember the candy lady that lived at the end of the street.

What was so cool about living on Basil Street was the fact that our grandmother lived right around the corner. Now I do remember that address because that's where we were most of the time and that was at 254 North Pine Street. What is so amazing is that the same house I pretty much grew up in is still there. Also Mrs. Ernestine who was our next-door neighbor who use to bath me as a little boy her house is still standing also.

Whenever I get a chance to go to Mobile and drive by there it brings back so many memories of growing up in a hard environment. This area was known for prostitution, drug use and gangs. It was to the point that you better not get caught coming across Davis Avenue after dark. And you really didn't play to far from your front door.

Times were hard then not only growing up there in the campground but how we grew up period. I can remember our grandmother taking us to a store named National or Big "D" as we called it and you could literally buy tennis shoes in the grocery store. They were on the shelves just like the cereal and as a kid in that area you felt good to go to the store and to be able to buy a pair of shoes even though you knew you were going to be made fun of because they were no name or Bo Bo's is what they used to call them.

You could hear gunshots ring out at night and would most certainly have to lock your doors and put the extra sliding lock on as well. I can see that green shotgun house now even as I am writing. Basically one front door and all the way at the other end of the house is the back door.

I can remember sometimes even having to eat cereal with water because there was no milk or if there was milk it was the powered welfare milk that made water taste better. Eating grilled cheese sandwiches made with government cheese that was so hard that it took hours just to melt it. On the TV there were just whatever channels you could get with rabbit ears with aluminum foil on the ends to try to help with reception.

What I can say now looking back is that even though we were in a hard environment I was able by the grace of God not to become a product of my environment when so many others were and I can only attribute that to my grandmother Mattie C. Simmons. She literally made us go to church, which of course was right in the center of the projects.

Most of us to be honest with you have come up in some type of hard environment. I know for me it was almost like being in a prison sometimes because you always had to watch over your shoulder. I remember one time when we were at my grandmother's house, a man came to the door and said his car broke down. Later that night when my grandmother was at church, Mr. Buddy who lived in the other room in the house, opened the door to this same guy who came back to our house.

We were in the one room that my grandmother and the rest of us stayed in and heard a scuffle and then a loud noise came to the door. My cousin opened the door. The man robbed us but didn't even see my grandmother's purse hanging on the door with money in it.

Eventually he left and when my grandmother got home we called my Uncle Sidney and he came with his shotgun. Well come to find out in the next room the noise we heard was Mr. Buddy being murdered. The man who came back to rob us, killed Mr. Buddy! It was only God that protected us from getting killed as well. In the room with me was my cousin and sister because we stayed home while our grandmother had went to church.

Growing up in a hard environment was just that - hard! Just thinking about that night from then on, knowing a man right in the next room was stabbed to death was mentally torturing because you didn't know if it would happen again. I can even now hear everybody crying and seeing the police lights shining down our street. Man, it was hard growing up in the campground.

Remember I said you better not get caught coming across Davis Avenue after dark? Well one night I did. I was trying to make it back to my grandmother's house coming from the projects. I had crossed Davis Avenue and out of no where someone grabbed my neck and snatched the gold chain I had on. Now I must note that this was no big expensive chain. It was a chain that I had got from Spencer Gifts.

I believe I ordered it from the Spencer Gifts magazine. Well I was not successful in stopping what was happening to me nor ran home or to my grandmother's telling my sisters what had happened. If you grew up in a hard environment I know this is probably having you to go down memory lane and probably is reminding you of some of the things you had to experience in your own journey.

What I can look back and be thankful for is that even though I grew up in a hard environment God didn't allow me to be a byproduct of my circumstance or what was going on around us. Some people's environments and circumstances affect them adversely. If I can share anything with you from my experience, it would be, God has a plan for you.

I say God has a plan for you because even now looking back nothing comes to mind of me making it through and out of my environment but God. I remember a time when my mother and her friend had begun to use drugs. There were needles all over the place. I was in the back and wanted to go to my Grandmother's house and they wouldn't let me. I cried and was so angry that I remember biting my hand because I was so mad and didn't want to be there with them doing what they were doing.

This was so hard to deal with as a child. I know that it was a result of hurt she must have had inside her from losing my father, which I will talk about later. Not everyone is born and raised in an environment of opulence. Some have journey's like mine and even yours. What I feel is important to know is you can be different in spite of your environment.

I can remember times where my mother would be beaten and jumped on by different men and what is so painful is I remember one time she was beaten so badly that her jaw was wired shut. You talk about a hard environment; man, this is certainly one. My hope is that my experience and journey will help you as you are on your journey of life and that it will provide a sense of encouragement and motivation for you.

Syrup sandwiches and buttered toast with sugar sprinkled on it was a normal thing. Wow, as I reminisce I kind of laugh even though it was not funny then. You just look back and realize how far God has brought you. I guess too, while you are in the environment you try your very best to make the best of it. I had a friend tell me that oatmeal is better than no meal. The point is something is better than nothing so truly in the end we can't complain.

I want you to receive this whether you have just come out of a hard environment or still in it. As you read this book, know this, that there is something so special about you that your situation can not take the fire out of your heart. What I am trying to say is I believe you will be able to make lemonade. You will take all that your hard environment is throwing at you, the sour and bitter and make lemonade out of it all.

Many have heard the saying, "You will not live to see eighteen." Well guess what? I am well pass eighteen. Growing up in Mobile was hard but I guess I was harder because I made it out and so can you. Now your hard environment may not be a city. It may be a relationship. It may be mentally, but whatever it is you will not be a byproduct of your environment.

I have to as they say, "Keep it Real" because sometimes I think people are ashamed of where they have had to come from and what they have had to endure. Wow, what just popped in my mind is, "It aint where you from it is where you at!" I know that may not be grammatically correct but nonetheless it is true. Keep pushing through your hard place.

Take everything that you have had to experience or may be experiencing now and use that as the fuel that allows you to keep traveling down the road of life because remember after all it is a journey.

Winding Road Ahead – Journal Moment

ROUGH ROAD

Chapter Two

Dealing with the Loss of My Father

The loudest screeching screams I have ever heard in my life rang out all over the house as my mom and my oldest sister come in shouting, "Daddy is dead!" At the age of nine years old how do you process that? How do you cope with such a painful and tragic situation? Your father has been murdered.

From what I can remember of my father he was a hard worker and a family man. I was told that I look just like him and that he was a sharp dresser. I believe he even spent some time in the military. I am going to try to make it through this chapter and not have tears flowing but you never get over something like this EVER! With God's help you just cope and the more years that go by you learn to cope a little better.

Samuel McGill, Jr., my dad, never got a chance to see me play in my high school basketball games. Never got a chance to give me that father-son talk right before going to my prom. Never got a chance to see me graduate and go into the Marine Corps. Thinking about it even now it is difficult dealing with the loss of my father.

It was such a convenience living right around the corner from my grandmother's house. It was so good because it was literally a five-minute or less walk. I know my dad loved me. I would love when he took us to K-Mart. I wish to this day that I had a picture of him but I don't. All I have is faint memories.

I can remember when a bad hurricane came through Mobile. I thought we were going to die, but my dad somehow kept the family together even in the midst of a storm. I remember after the hurricane had passed we had this old manual washing machine that had the wringer on top and a rat I mean a big rat got into the washer. I could see my dad taking this big stick and killing it. I couldnot have done that…LOL

He was a champion and a real man. His nickname was Peanut. I don't know why they called him that but I remember everyone calling him by that name and of course we had to call him daddy. It wasn't something a child did; calling your parents by their first name. I just really remember him as always being a hard worker and a provider.

I would give the world to have a picture of him. I know he loved my mom and my mom loved him just as equally hard if not harder. I am honored that I was the son that was named after him. To have the name Samuel McGill, III is a badge of honor to me especially since everyone use to tell me all the time that you look just like Peanut.

One night when we where at my grandmother's house my oldest sister got in trouble and my grandmother sent her home to our house. When she got there my mom and dad and their friends who were another male and female couple were going out and since they had no choice they had to take my sister with them. While they were riding, it was later told to me they stopped at the Kentucky Fried Chicken right at the corner, I believe of Ann Street and Government Boulevard there in Mobile, Alabama.

From that moment on things would never be the same. My father's friend went in to place the order but apparently couldn't make up his mind on what to get and was trying to motion for his girlfriend to come in but she didn't see him. By this time he is enraged and comes out and begins to jump on her and beat her.

My father was outmatched in size and was desperate to get the man off the lady. So he goes to the trunk and gets a crowbar to try to get him off her and that's when everything went south. The man got the crowbar from my dad and begins to beat him literally to death. LITERALLY!

Blood was everywhere and the ambulance was called. My dad was in the back of the ambulance as it was speeding down the road with sirens blazing. But when they got to the hospital they pronounced him DOA, which is Dead on Arrival. My father had been taken from me never to return back.

Meanwhile as this is happening my other siblings and I are at our grandmother's not knowing what is happening until the front door opens and the loudest screeching screams I have ever heard in my life ring out all over the house as my mom and my oldest sister come in shouting, "Daddy is dead!" My mom and oldest sister collapse and now are on the floor crying and my life would never be the same.

I don't remember crying that night. Maybe it didn't set in what had actually happened. This was a night that no one saw coming. It was one of the worst nights of my life.

As I think about it now tears are building up in my eyes because you never get over something like this. As I fore stated God just helps you to cope year after year. I often asked why my dad. Now funeral arrangements have to be made and as a young kid I remember my dad's family coming from Connecticut and New York.

I can't remember any faces but I remember my aunt on my dad's side which was his sister being there and finding out she was the one who gave me my nickname. I know you want me to tell you what it is. Ok my nickname is Pookie. Well for you Bishop Samuel McGill, III…LOL

Everyone is now in town and the funeral is commencing and for the first time I saw my father in the casket. I can't remember now actually what he looked like and maybe that is for a reason but even then, I don't remember crying. I could hear everyone else crying and sobbing. What also is strange is I don't remember anything about the graveside portion of the funeral. However, I do remember my mom getting a flag because of his military service.

I guess the question is how do you deal with the loss of your father? Honestly I think I still deal with it in whatever way because there are times I say to myself I wonder what my father would be saying and how he would be feeling about some of my life's accomplishments. I wonder what advise he would have given me when I have had situations where I needed a father's wisdom.

Many of you reading this may have lost your father and know exactly what I mean and how I feel. It is something that never goes away.

Times like Father's Day are times that I wish he was here and when you achieve something there is nothing like having your dad to say that he is proud of you. I know I will never ever have that because he was taken away from me. My brother and sisters probably have their own way of dealing with our loss. I still wish he were here.

Even after his funeral, for a long time the bloodstains were still there at the Kentucky Fried Chicken and I didn't like passing by that way even though I was not physically there when all this happened. I just didn't like going by there. None of us ate at that KFC again. To answer the question that may be going through some of your minds, yes I eat KFC now.

I did find something out that was interesting about my father from my Uncle Rod. My dad was in the choir. I hope he could sing a whole lot better than I can. I am laughing because I know I can't sing! I sound good to myself. I miss my dad very much and can only hope that the legacy I leave behind will be one that honors his name.

I know everything that I am comes from him including his work ethic. Loving to dress and looking nice came from him and I heard he was a handsome fellow too. Yes, you know I am smiling about that. Dealing with the loss of my father is something I never could have imagined nor something I would have to speak about. I do know that we can make it. It is tough but sometimes this is one of the rough roads that life has us travel down.

Rough Road — Journal Moment

ROUGH CROSSING

Chapter Three

Dealing with the Loss of My Son

As though the loss of my father wasn't enough here I am now at another rough crossing. This is something that no parent wants to have to deal with but especially as a young new parent. I never could have imagined that I would have to go through something like this. Yes, I am talking about the loss of my first-born son whose name was Derrick Trevon Watts-McGill.

I don't even know where to begin. This is a tender spot in my heart and life. I was dating this young lady and was head over hills in love with her and would do anything for her. I use to run miles just to get to her house to see her. Looking back, I would have to say that she was my first love.

I went to Shaw High School in Columbus, Georgia and she went to Kendrick High School. I was on the basketball team and it was a good thing not having a girlfriend that went to my same school besides that it was just good simply because she meant the world to me. Well you all knew this was coming. I had to get in good with her dad who was a U.S. Marine.

I had one thing going for me and that is we both had the same first name and an extra bonus was that I was going to be going into the Marines after graduation. It was my senior year and I was already enrolled in the delayed entry program with the Marines and was excited to go even though all my friends thought I was crazy and said that the Marines would do nothing but brain wash me. They could say what they wanted to I was going and fired up about it.

Things with my girlfriend and me were good and to me there was nothing that we had any issue with. Prom time was coming up and of course I asked her to go to my prom, which was my senior prom, and the first time I had went to prom because I wanted to wait until my last year and enjoy it then.

I had the perfect tuxedo with tails. It was white with pink cummerbund and tie and oh yes I had the cane also. Man, you couldn't tell me anything! I was sharp and she was stunningly beautiful. I had already worked it out with my recruiter to take his nice black 5.0 Mustang. The evening was just right. When I picked her up I was like wow. Of course, her dad gave me the speech on what time to have her back home.

Well you know when you are not saved you do things. I must admit that when we got there we took pictures and danced for a little bit and was out of there to eat and then to the hotel room. Well don't judge me because some of you went to the hotel room too after prom…LOL

This was our first time ever being intimately involved. I did have protection but it broke and I didn't even realize it but I never thought that she would end up pregnant; but guess what I was wrong. So, the lesson is, it truly only takes one time. Well we got dressed and left the hotel because remember her dad have given me the speech on the time to have her back and he was a very intimidating man and a Marine at that so you best believe I was pulling up to her house at the time I was told.

He had no idea what we had done and I was certainly not going to say anything either. As time went by she called me and told me that she was pregnant so I told her that I would take her to a clinic so that we can make sure because sometimes pregnancy test cannot be accurate. The pregnancy test was accurate and the test at the clinic confirmed that.

What do we do now because I am scared and so was she? Now I had to break this news to her parents and I know they would not be happy. You can imagine how nervous I was, about to graduate from high school and go off into the Marines and having to tell this man who was tough as nails; I was petrified. Nevertheless, I mustered up enough courage to tell her parents.

    Her Dad was so disappointed. I believe he was more disappointed in us than he was mad and her mother shared those same feelings. I expressed to them without hesitation that I love their daughter and was going to do what I had to do as the father to be a provider and a father to our child and I meant just that because as my first love there was nothing I would not have done for her.

    I remember the day before I left we were together and I thought things were so good and I knew I was going to be gone for three months of rigorous training in Marine Corps Boot Camp there at Parris Island, SC but to me our relationship was where it would be ok plus we are going to be having a child together. So off to boot camp I go.

    When we got to Charleston, SC these Marine Drill Instructors come up to us all who are going to boot camp and in our face shout, "Get up against the wall" and man I was like what did I get myself into. They loaded us onto this bus and seemed like rode us around all night until we began to drift off to sleep and the next thing I remembered as I woke up was seeing this red and yellow sign that said Marine Corps Recruit Depot, Parris Island, South Carolina. The bus pulled up to this building and oh my goodness.

This short D.I. (Drill Instructor) got on the bus and starting shouting, "Get off my bus!" As we got off the bus we had to get on these yellow footprints and yes I am saying now, "What did I get myself into!" I know for at least 48 hours we were not allowed to sleep. It was so hard staying up but they immediately began to have us in war mode and didn't let up at all.

If you got caught drifting off to sleep the D.I. would smack the back of your head so hard it made you think twice about dozing off again. If you were walking they would just shout, "Freeze Recruit, Freeze!" and whatever position you were in that's where you had better stay. One guy's foot was up in the air when that was yelled one time and he didn't keep it there but allowed it to come down to the ground.

The Drill Instructors all ran to him and said, "You just stepped on a land mine and blew all of us up!" Man, this truly was the real deal. They were getting every bit of civilian lifestyle and mindset out of us and preparing us to be warriors. I was selected as a squad leader, which means I was responsible for the lives of other individuals but looking back I see God's preparation even in this responsibility.

This was a culture shock to say the least.

Well there came a time where we could finally write and my girlfriend was the first one that I wrote as well as my aunt Jean (Martha Thirkield). Well when I got a letter from her (my girlfriend) it was a letter saying that she had moved on. That crushed me and I just turned over my foot locker and was so upset that my Senior D.I. asked if I needed to call home which doesn't happen and I said yes.

When I got her on the phone she talked to me like I was a dog. I had to pull it together because I only had a few more weeks until graduation and I would be home on leave until time to go to my M.O.S. School. When I got there to see her stomach showing so big made me forget about how she was treating me and what she had done.

Well the time had come now that I had to go to my military occupational specialty school, which was at Camp Lejeune, NC. Again, I had to leave but I was still happy that I was going to be a dad and knew that it was going to be a boy. Well even though she did what she did and had moved on for whatever her reasons were, it made me no mind because it got back to me that she was at the football game in this guy's lap carrying my child.

I had to stay focus there at M.O.S. School and I still was nice and cordial to her for my son's sake. Well as normal I would call to check up on her and the baby but something was not normal this time. Her mom answered the phone, which she rarely did. When I asked to speak to my girlfriend her mom said that she was in the hospital.

That was not good because I knew she had several more weeks before she was due so I asked what was going on and she told me that they admitted her in the hospital and the baby was born prematurely and was in ICU and they said that he was not going to make it because they had him on the life support. Every day he had been losing weight.

I was literally stunned and immediately put in for emergency leave and went back to Columbus, Georgia and headed straight for the hospital. When I got there, this is what I saw.

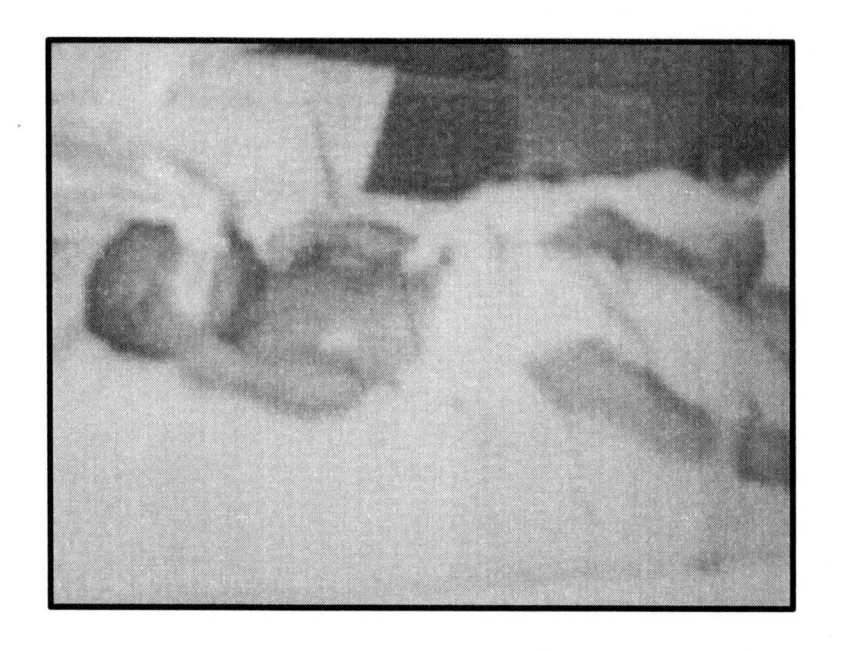

My son in ICU connected to the life support, breathing machine and other wires connected to him. They since he has been born he had never opened his eyes. This was so much for me to take in and process. As I was there with him I took my finger and placed it near his hand and he grabbed my finger and held it.

I could remember my grandmother praying all the time and going to bed seeing her kneeled by her bed and praying and when I woke up she was still in that same position. Even though I didn't have a relationship with God I started to pray and ask God to allow me to see his eyes. As soon as I said that for the very first time he opened his eyes and looked at me. I miss him even now. This was a rough crossing in my journey and I guess we all have those times in our journey where it is rough trying to cross certain times in our lives.

This was a lot for me to take and knowing I had to get back because my leave was almost up was another level of stress. The doctors called us into a private waiting room area to let us know that my son was only alive because of the life support-breathing machine and was still losing weight and ask us what we wanted to do.

His options were leave him on the life support knowing that he was rapidly losing weight every day or take him off the life support system and allow as he said, "Nature to take its course." Well this was one of the toughest decision I had to make or be involved in making. We decided to have him taken off the life support but I told them not to do it while I was there but to immediately call me if anything happened.

When I left the hospital, and began driving back to my aunt's house I could not even get there good before my phone rang and they informed me to come back to the hospital because my son had died. Even now it is hard to even begin to describe that feeling. Losing my father now my first born and only son was something that crushed my heart.

They said that he had Trisomy 13 which was a rare chromosomal disorder in which all or portion of chromosome 13 appears three times (trisomy) rather than twice in cells of the body. This baffled me because nothing like this ever was in my family. To add to the pain, I now had to get back to M.O.S. School there in Camp Lejeune, North Carolina because my emergency leave was up and we were also receiving orders to our first duty stations. Still devastated and hurt come to find out that my orders were sending me to Okinawa, Japan as my first duty station.

I was so hurt by the loss of my son that I didn't talk to anyone for three months. I didn't talk at all unless I had to, (in connection with) my military responsibilities. I'm now in a country I had never been in before going through a rough crossing in my life and it was so difficult. I don't even know how I made through each day.

I did want to make sure that it was nothing on my end that had to do with this chromosomal disorder that took my sons life so I went to the doctor there on base and they did a chromosomal test and it came back all clear for me.

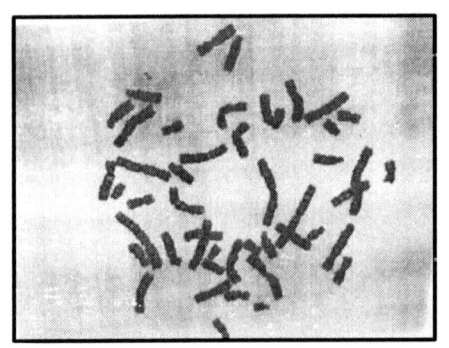

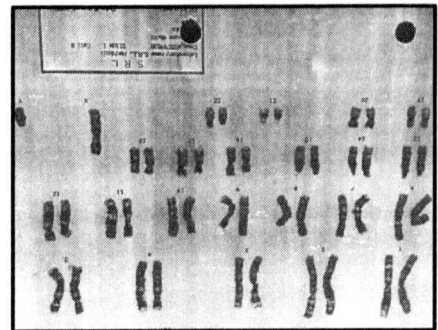

The above are the actual images of my chromosomes that I still have from my military records. Even though the test cleared me as far as seeing if it was something that would be a concern with future children it didn't bring my son back.

I am not sure that if the mother of my child ever got tested because after my son's death that relationship deteriorated because for me my son only held it together. She had already shown me what she was about by what she did while I was in boot camp.

My son would have been twenty-five years old now had he lived. In life, you will not always get the answers to your questions. In times like these, I can only tell you to trust God when you can't understand why. Maybe God knew that it would be hard for me to take care of him and all the possible medical needs he may have had. I don't know but as the saying goes, "You will understand it better by and by."

Rough Crossing — Journal Moment

DETOUR

Chapter Four

The Brig

A deviation from the normal course is the definition of the word detour. If we are honest, all of us at some point has deviated from where we were supposed to be going, present company included. After the loss of my son and being stationed in Okinawa, Japan, my first duty station had its effect on me.

When I got back to the States my duty station was Camp Lejeune, North Carolina where I had been for my M.O.S. School. Well I was not saved and did a lot of partying and clubbing. I carried my gun with me everywhere I went. My 9MM was my best friend. I carried that gun because I thought that I looked good and was not going to tussle with anyone. I was going to shoot first and then ask questions later.

The place to be was always the Enlisted Club, City Lights Club or the Talk of the Town and I was one that hit them all. Drinking and partying was something I did on the regular. Maybe it was a way that I dealt with all of what I had faced and dealt with but I am not Dr. Phil and can't say why I did those things back then. I just did. I was just off course.

I had this white Hyundai Excel and back then it was a bad ride. I had chrome rims and a booming sound system and finally was voted in as a member of the local car club, which was Low Level Finest. Man, you couldn't tell me anything.

As normal routine, I would go out to the clubs. Something would happen this night that detoured my life in a major way. I went to the E-Club (Enlisted Club) located on Camp Geiger and yes had my gun with me. It was a little cold because I remember having on jeans and a sweater and my gun was hiding underneath my sweater.

Already a little tipsy someone tried to start a fight and I pulled my gun out on him and of course a piece brings about peace. I got in my car and headed off base, but when I got to the front gate the MP's (Military Police) pulled me over and asked me if I had a gun and of course I lied and said no.

They searched me and found the gun loaded with 19 rounds in the clip and 1 in the chamber of the gun. Well I don't have to tell you what happened next. Yes, they immediately arrested me. The charges piled up on me and I ended up being court martialed. A special court martial is what they gave me.

Regardless of the offenses involved, a special court-martial sentence is limited to no more than forfeiture of two-thirds basic pay per month for one year, and additionally for enlisted personnel, one year confinement (or a lesser amount if the offenses have a lower maximum), and/or a bad-conduct discharge.

So now I am in custody awaiting my trial to begin and the military prosecutor was trying to throw the book at me to include the reduction in rank, forfeiture in pay and a BCD in which we called a Big Chicken Dinner or as it is really known; a Bad Conduct Discharge.

A Bad Conduct Discharge would have most certainly messed me up for life. What do I do now? Well I was assigned a defense attorney and the process began. When I say, the prosecutor was trying to throw everything at me including the kitchen sink that is exactly what he was trying to do.

Here is the part you must catch and that is my service record was impeccable. I was a well decorated Marine to include Meritorious Mast as well as Letters of Accommodations and the list goes on. Well having seen this in my records the Judge who was a Full Bird Colonel asked me, "What are you doing in my court room?"

He further said we are going to take a recess and when we come back I am handing down my sentence. Well I know this could mean loss of rank, money and being dishonorably discharged from the Marines Corps. I did not have a bone fide relationship with the Lord, but I began to pray. My prayer went like this, "Lord I don't know what you want with me but if you allow me to stay in the Marines and not be dishonorably discharged I will listen to what you have to say."

Well when the recess was over and everyone assembled back inside the courtroom. The judge said, "I'm not going to discharge you." When he said that I knew God had heard my prayer. He did however reduce me in rank, forfeiture my pay and sentence me to 120 days confinement in the Military Brig.

My life had gotten off course but God had a plan for my life and I was off to the brig.

The brig was no joke and certainly not a vacation. When I got to the intake section it was nothing I could have ever prepared for or imagined. The guards immediately called me prisoner and you could not make direct eye contact with them. All my civilian clothes I had on at that time were taken and I was given prison orange. I don't care what anyone says, orange is not the new black.

Well my attitude was much different by this time. Remember I was praying at the trial Lord if you allow me to stay in the Marines I will listen to what you say. I was like I am just going to do my time get out. I planned on business as usual but little did I know something was going to happen. It would forever change my life and I am so glad that it did.

Being in the brig was something totally shocking. Number one your freedom was gone. Then you had to be locked up in a squad bay dorm type setting with about 10 – 15 other prisoners (Marines). Having to shower with other men at the same time was like crazy and you best not drop your soap as they say.

You were no longer your own you had to take orders and be called prisoner and if you had a visitor they had to strip search and cavity search you which was degrading. I remember one day just putting a chit or request in the chaplain's box and asking for a Bible and when I got it I started reading it.

I mean I read it from cover to cover. I remember reading the Bible all the time. When others would play basketball for their yard time, I would read my Bible. I carried that Bible everywhere I could take it and stayed in it.

I read the entire Old Testament and then the New Testament. I remember clearly reading Acts 2:38-42 which said, "Then Peter said unto them, repent, and be baptized every one of you in the name of Jesus Christ for the remission of sins, and ye shall receive the gift of the Holy Ghost. For the promise is unto you, and to your children, and to all that are afar off, even as many as the Lord our God shall call. And with many other words did he testify and exhort, saying, save yourselves from this untoward generation."

I also remember Acts 1:8 saying, "But ye shall receive power, after that the Holy Ghost is come upon you: and ye shall be witnesses unto me both in Jerusalem, and in all Judaea, and in Samaria, and unto the uttermost part of the earth." I wanted exactly what I was reading about. So, I put in a chit again in the Chaplain's box but this time I was requesting to be baptized.

I said to myself if anybody come in here and try to baptize me any other way than what I read I was going to leave them in the water by themselves. The time came for me to be baptized and I remember these two brothers coming and there was this wooden box filled with water but only one person could fit in it and I had to curl up in the fetal position just to fit in the box. The two brothers that came were Brother Vernon Miller and Elder Larry Davidson.

They began to read from Romans 6 and Acts 2 like I did, so I said to myself this is it. They were outside the box and took me and said, "Brother McGill upon the confession of your faith in the death, burial and resurrection of our Lord and Savior Jesus Christ we are going to baptize you in the name of Jesus Christ for the remission of your sins and you shall receive the gift of the Holy Ghost for it is a promise unto you, your children and as many as are afar off as many as the Lord our God shall call as we baptize you in Jesus name."

Once they said that they took me down in the water but my foot came up because the box was so small and they said we must take you down again because you need to be completely covered under water. And they said, "we baptize you in Jesus name" and took me down again and this time I was completely covered under the water. When I came up out of the water this time I felt different. I couldn't explain it but I knew something had happened.

After being baptized I kept reading the bible both day and night. I started reading about the Holy Ghost. I started seeing where people received the Holy Ghost evidenced by speaking in other tongues as the Spirit gave them utterance and I said I want that! One night when lights were out I got down on my knees by my bunk and started praying and felt something in my throat. It scared me so I jumped in my bunk and went to sleep.

That same night I had a dream and in the dream, it was as though I was looking down at myself. In the dream like I was watching a movie. In the dream, I was lying in my bunk and the ceiling opened and flames of fire started to descend upon my body and when the flames hit my body I started in the dream speaking in tongues and I woke up. Later that day I placed yet another chit (request) to go to the chapel church service. I will never ever forget this day.

When I got to the chapel it was a man by the name of brother Steve from the UPC (United Pentecostal Church) that said if there is anyone here that wants something from God to come to the altar and might I say the church services were held in the upper room, which was on the very top floor of the brig. I ran to the altar because I wanted the Holy Ghost like I read about in the Bible.

When I got to the altar I closed my eyes and totally blocked out everything around me and started calling on the only name of Jesus. As I called on Jesus something happened that would forever change my life. As I kept calling that wonderful name I could feel the same fire I saw in my dream I could feel it in my hands and it traveled down my arms, down my chest and all the way down my legs and when it hit my feet I heard this wonderful heavenly language that I had never heard before in my life.

It was the most beautiful distinct language that flowed like a mighty river. By now the guard is tapping me on my shoulder and told me that I had been there now for thirty minutes and the service was dismissed thirty minutes ago and that I had to go back to my cell. As I began to take my first step I began to stagger as a person would who was intoxicated. Well I wasn't drunk but I was certainly filled with the Holy Ghost. I knew it and the devil did too.

As I got back to my cell, the other brothers knew I had it too. I can say my life has never been the same. For someone reading this that may wonder if God is real; I am a living witness to tell you that not only is Jesus real but he is the best thing that has ever happen to me.

From that moment on as I read the Bible it was so much clearer to me. It seems like revelation jumped off the pages like never before. Whenever anyone had a question about the Bible they would find me to ask me to explain it or one of the other brothers they knew who were saved. This was so amazing that they would do that. Every time someone had a question the Lord would give me such wisdom and clarity that it truly was amazing seeing him use me like that. Little did I know he was preparing me for ministry even then and I had no idea of what was happening.

Once I had received the Holy Ghost even though I was still locked up I had such a feeling of freedom that was so liberating and amazing. Truly whom the Son has made free is free indeed. At this part of my journey I may have deviated from the normal course that I was on, but truly the steps of a good man are ordered by the Lord and he delights in his way.

Detour – Journal Moment

STOP

Chapter Five

Wounded in the Church

It has been said that church hurt is the worst kind of hurt to experience. Well I want to talk about this a little because first the church has never done anything to us but provide a way of escape for the believers. It is the church as an institution that Jesus is coming back for. I do believe it is the people that are in the church that we, sadly to say, are wounded by.

Zechariah 13:6 says, "And one shall say unto him, what are these wounds between thine arms? Then he shall answer, those with which I was wounded in the house of my friends." Never indict the church as an institution for what an individual or individuals may have done or said to you that hurt you. Truth is people have said stuff to us on our jobs that we didn't like or hurt us but we didn't go around quitting or walking away from jobs because of people, so let's not do that when it comes to the church of Jesus Christ.

I too have experienced church hurt, but I have always had a philosophy that I was not going to let anyone separate me from the love of Christ. Sometimes you must stop and look at what you are allowing to get to you in the house of God. When you look at it, often it isn't even worth your time. I don't mean to sound cold or callous but is there anything someone can do or say that will keep you away from God's house?

My answer to that question is, "I don't think so!"

This is so funny and when he reads this he will probably laugh like I am right now as I am writing this. Well one of my closest friends Elder Ivan Elam back in the day we both were brought before the church like criminals being brought before a firing squad. Falsely accused and everything. The funny thing is when we looked around the person that should have been standing there was not even brought forward.

We laugh about it even to this very day. I mean we were put on public display and were innocent. Now that could have damaged us but instead of allowing it to, we used it to our advantage because when you know the truth you never have to defend a lie. We took it in stride and can now look back and hurt ourselves laughing at that event that could have caused most people to walk away from God but again, who shall separate us from the Love of Christ?

I think too that sometimes wounds or hurt comes from having a higher expectation of someone. That places us in a position where we can be wounded or even sometimes taken advantage of and hurt. I believe often we place the people of God and preachers whether men or woman on pedestals or above being human. Someone needs to hear this because you have been hanging on to the hurt that you have experienced years ago that just so happened to have taken place in the church.

I have come to learn that forgiveness is the most powerful thing that you can release or give a person because it keeps you and I from imprisoning ourselves and stopping our growth and advancement in the kingdom of our God. Pain is never enjoyable when you are going through it but there is something wonderful about the other side that makes it worth not staying stuck in the now of the hurt. How do I get over the hurt you might ask?

I think for any wound to heal you have to first not cover it up and then you have to not pick with it. God is a healer of the heart and I want to applaud you for staying with Jesus even after being hurt in the church or the building because remember the church, as an institution is awesome.

We are striving for perfection and will get there if we keep pushing towards it.

The flip side to the coin is maybe we have caused hurt to someone in the church as well. I think we do well when we have offended someone to go to that person and try to reconcile and get things right. Where it gets off at times is when we go to everyone but the party or parties involved in the situation. Man, that's when it gets crazy.

Remember the Bible says in Matthew 5:23, "Therefore if thou bring thy gift to the altar, and there rememberest that thy brother hath ought against thee; Leave there thy gift before the altar, and go thy way; first be reconciled to thy brother, and then come and offer thy gift." I think that if we just handle things the way the Bible says, we will have less offense and hurt in the church.

Also, we need to be willing to give and receive forgiveness because bitterness is a serious thing that can build up in us subtly if we do not keep a heart of forgiveness. Now, I am not saying be a door mat to people but I am saying, (I have had to do this myself) and that is, let things go that are not worth holding on to because they only end up slowing you down.

Stop for a moment and think is there any wounds that you are holding on to that you should let go of right now. If so, just say that to pain and hurt, I release you in Jesus name and no longer will I carry you around. Now doesn't that feel a whole lot better?

No matter what road our journey takes us down, there is always something we can learn from. What we experienced, we take those experiences and use them to make us a better person. We've cried too many tears to count but if it made you better, it was worth it even if it didn't feel like it at that present time. Wounded but still here. That's right let me say that again, "Wounded but still here!" The devil thought that he could get you to quit but look at you with your bad self....LOL

I want to say thank you for yet pressing forward in your life despite of hurt, pain and disappointments because of your perseverance someone else will be blessed and gain strength by you not throwing in the towel. What we go through is always for someone else to benefit from. Thank you for being a champion and taking what happened to you and used it for God's glory over your life.

Wounded in the church but still here!!!

Stop — Journal Moment

ROAD CLOSED

Chapter Six

Burying My Mother

When a road is closed that means you can't use that road whether temporarily or permanent. Well this closed road I am going to attempt to go back down to share with you is what I remember of the life of Augustine McGill. That's right this road leads me to a place that yet again was one I never thought I would have to experience and that is to have to bury my mother.

As far back as I can remember my mom was always the one who took care of my sisters, brother and I. She was the one who was home taking care of everything. My dad, from what I can remember was the bread and worked and as they old saying goes he brought home the bacon.

I don't ever remember my mother having a job, seem like taking care of us was her fulltime job; cooking, cleaning and making sure her kids were reared and she did it well. One thing I can say is that she loved my father with all her heart. When my father was killed right in front of her eyes, that affected her so bad that she spiraled downhill and started drinking and doing drugs and other things that you wouldn't want your mother to be involved with doing.

One of the benefits she had was that we lived around the corner from her mom's, which of course was my grandmother Mattie C. Simmons. Whenever her and my dad wanted to go out she would take us to our grandmother's house. One night, we were already at my grandmother's and my oldest sister had gotten into trouble and my grandmother sent her home to our house around the corner. When she got there my parents and another couple were getting ready to go out. Since they had nowhere else for my sister to go they had to take her with them.

As they were out, the other man got hungry and said he wanted something to eat. So, they stopped at a Kentucky Fried Chicken and the guy got out and went in to get some food. Apparently, he could not make up his mind what he wanted to eat and was trying to motion for his girlfriend. She didn't see him beckoning for her and he got upset to the point of reckless rage and came out and began to beat her.

My father trying to do the best he could to stop what was going on, but was outmatched in size compared to this guy. He went to the trunk and got a crowbar as a desperate act to prevent serious injuries to the lady but as I fore stated in an earlier chapter that is where things went south and ultimately it ended up in my father's fatality. By the time they got my father to the hospital he was already dead.

My mother was not able to handle this and that's when things for her spiraled downhill in her life. She started to drink, do drugs and even prostitution. We never know how people handle certain things and this per her reactive behavior says it totally and completely devastated her because I never saw her drink, do drugs and certainly not sell her body before.

I was around the age of nine years old when all of this happened and what I remember next is my aunt Jean coming to Mobile to buy grandmother's house and she asked me if I wanted to come to her house in Columbus, Georgia and I said yes because I thought it was a summer thing. When I got there, it was not what I was used to because she had this huge split level house and HBO which I had never even knew what HBO and Showtime was and here I was now in what seemed like the lap of luxury.

Time went on and the next thing I knew I was being enrolled in school. My aunt began to take good care of me. Meanwhile my mom had gotten so bad. She even got beat one time and it was so bad that her month had to be wired shut. Years went by and it was as though she became a wonderer going from here to there.

As I got older I would go to Mobile to try to find her and it would sometimes be like trying to find a needle in a haystack. I would go to each neighborhood "Hit House" that was the places or the house where they would drink and get high and play cards and all sorts of other things. Sometimes I would find her and other times I wouldn't.

I remember very vividly being in the Marines Corps and being stationed in Okinawa, Japan and getting word that a car had hit her. Of course, I took an emergency leave and took a 13-hour flight back to the States to try to find out what happened to her. When I got back, I had to do the normal search for her only to find out that she had been arrested and was in jail.

By the time I got to the courthouse and searched there, I found out that she had been released earlier. I go to each hit house and find her this time and I told her that she was coming with me.

She told me that she was with her friends and to come back. I did, only to find her again.

Knowing I had only so much time on this emergency leave, I told everybody in the hit house that once I come back she better be here or I was going to shoot up everything in that house. I must have sacred all of them to death because when I came back she was there and said her usual which, was, "Baby, buy your momma some cigarettes."

I remember buying her a dress and of course the cigarettes because how do you tell your momma no. I loved her. We spent the day together and eventually I had to go back to Japan. She was still fighting mentally what had happened to my father because she was still doing what she had been for years; drink.

I remember on another occasion coming to Mobile to find her. When I did, she was walking down the street. I pulled my car over quickly and ran up to her only to be left standing there in the street as she walked off. That hurt me so bad I got back to the car and began to cry. I hated seeing her like that.

Years went by and I didn't see or hear anything from her but would always pray for her and ask God to keep her alive until I could see her. By this time, I was saved and preaching. I asked God to not let anything happen to her until she could hear her son preach. My Aunt had passed which was her sister and the family had asked me to do the funeral.

As I was preaching I could look out into the crowd and see her sitting next to my baby sister and see my sister pointing at me. Later, I told myself she was telling my mom that's your oldest son. She didn't even know it was me. This is a picture of us from that day.

Augustine McGill and Samuel McGill III her oldest son. Wow, seems like just yesterday this picture was taken.

God answered my prayer. She did hear me preach even though it was her sister's funeral.

Even though my mom's journey took her down the road. I can say in my heart that she loved me and not only me, but also all her children. I can tell by the display of affection in one of the last pictures that I took with her, which is below.

She loved me and I know she would brag on me. Just looking at the picture brings tears to my eyes because I know this was the last picture that I would ever take with her. Not too long after this picture I got a call that I was not prepared for, nor did I want.

One night while at home. I got a call from one of my cousins that said your mom is in the hospital and has died. When I heard that, it was as though the breath was knocked out of me and I started crying and breathing as though I was hyperventilating. It knocked me literally to my knees. My youngest sister arrived at the hospital and called me. I can tell you now this was in fact one of the toughest times of my life.

I now must take the lead amongst my siblings to do the following: make funeral arrangements, pay for the funeral, arrange the church to have the funeral, get a burial plot and preach the funeral too. Yes, I preached the funeral. Looking back, I know it was only God that gave me the strength to do all of this. I have to give Reverend Parrish and Nazarene Baptist Church for allowing me to have the funeral there. What was special about that church is it was the one we went to when we were little. My grandmother had such a profound legacy with this church and this is where my grandmother took us.

The saints of that church were so kind and even today I am eternally grateful. Not in a million years would I have known that not only would I have preached my Aunt Bessie's funeral but also her sister and my mom Augustine's funeral as well. Having to bury my mom was for me a road closing in my life. Some questions I left unanswered. For instance, I could never get the strength to have the autopsy report sent to me.

Maybe one day I will, but something in me didn't want to know the cause of death because of how rough her life was from the time of my father's murder. What could the possible cause be? I feel a peace in my heart because I believe she had made her peace with God and gave him her life and that is the memory I have and will forever hold on to. I love Augustine McGill and always will.

Road Closed – Journal Moment

BUMP

Chapter Seven

Time and Chance (Hotel Experience)

Ecclesiastes 9:11 says, "I returned, and saw under the sun, that the race is not to the swift, nor the battle to the strong, neither yet bread to the wise, nor yet riches to men of understanding, nor yet favor to men of skill; but time and chance happeneth to them all." The part I want to highlight is, "Time and chance happeneth to them all."

One translation of that text says, "For time and chance overtake them all." In other words, life happens to the best of us. This is the part of my journey that I look at as a bump in the road. There was a period in my life where I said to myself, "It can't get any worse than this!" Well it did. Things had gotten so bad. Jobs were hard to find and I could no longer afford my apartment and ended up in an Extended Stay Motel 6.

You talk about a bump in the road. Oh, my goodness! It was a small hotel room that had the small kitchenette in the room. I barely could pay for the room from week to week and there was no filet mignon to eat. It was Ramen noodles and hot pockets daily. That's probably why to this day I don't like either. I mean it was hard and at the time I didn't even have a car.

And the crazy thing about it all is I believe I was still hosting Christian television and no one knew what I was going through. Can you imagine that going through this bump in life and still smiling and being in front of a camera encouraging everybody else? Looking back, I believe that while I was encouraging others somehow the Lord was encouraging me. I must honor one of my dearest friends and big sister in the Lord and that is Dr. Pauline Key because she would come by and pick me up and take me wherever I needed to go whether it was to the store or just to get out of that small hotel room. When I say small I mean small.

That is what real friends do and I can say to her thank you Dr. Pauline Key you don't know how much coming to get me in those times kept me sane. I do remember having my laptop and like a true entrepreneur I felt like as long as I have this laptop and internet access I am going to make some money. I was pressing forward even though it seemed like I had hit a bump in the road.

Some people when they hit a bump in their journey, it derails them but somehow I keep pressing and telling life this is not my final destination. I had a push in me that I was not going to let anything kill out or destroy. I guess the result I saw for myself was bigger than what life was trying to show me at that time. I don't want you to think that I was solely operating off my own strength because that is simply not the case. As the saying goes, "If it had not been for the Lord who was on my side, where would I be?"

I want to say that when we see people in certain situations in life let's no judge them harshly because time and chance happens to us all. The question was asked, "What happened?" The response was, "Life happened!" We never know how people got to where they are in life perhaps they have hit a bump in the road of their journey.

For example, every person that is homeless is not at that place because they want to be. Life throws blows that sometimes can knock you to your lowest point. I just want to encourage you and say that when life knocks you down even though it feels like you can't you can get up! Not only can you get up but also you can achieve everything you have in your heart. I am a living witness and example of the power of God that can restore and give you double for your trouble.

Whatever you do, stay on the road! Life is a journey and the only way to make it to the final destination is stay on the road no matter what. We don't all experience the same things in life, but this I do know we can do all things through Christ that gives us the strength. So, as you are reading this know that God feels what you are going through and dealing with and he will always be there when it seems like others aren't.

Being in that motel room not knowing how I was going to pay for it from week to week certainly makes me look back a appreciate where God has allowed me to make it to at this time in my life. Thank you, Jesus! To go from walking to now driving a Mercedes Benz is a testimony. I don't mention that to brag or think I am something. I just want you to know if he did it for me why can't he do it for you?

Time and chance happens to us all. Next time you see a homeless person or someone less fortunate than you just whisper a quick prayer for them. I remember days in that motel room were harder than others but something in me would not allow me to be satisfied with where I was. A good friend of mine told me it was because I had drive. Well, I want to remind you that even though it doesn't feel like it, I believe you have drive. I speak to the drive in you now and remind you that everything you need is inside you. Sometimes we need people to remind us of what we already know. You are a champion and you will succeed even on your most difficult days and trust me they do come no matter who we are or what we have. Life happens.

I just want you to remember these words; "Wherever you are on your journey it is not the end for you." Keep pressing because trouble doesn't last always and even though it rains, the sun eventually comes shining through again. I look back now and say wow. Know that if you stay on the road you do travel past situations that at the current time you don't feel like you would make it through. Even know if I lost it all I gained something so much more valuable and that is having a more deep and intimate relationship with God because the truth of the matter is I would not have made it through anything without him.

Bump — Journal Moment

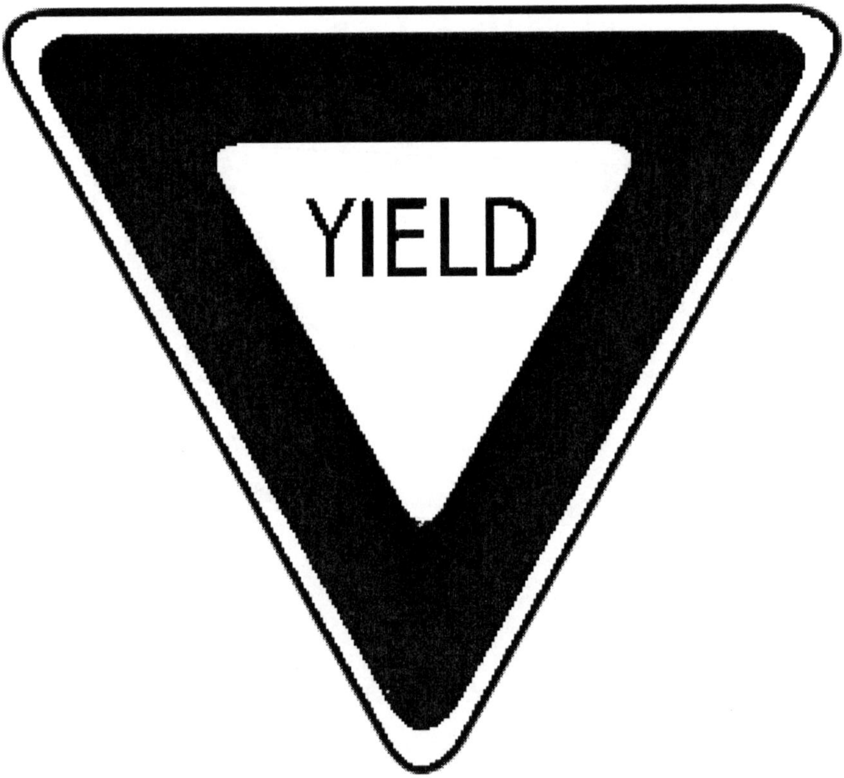
YIELD

Chapter Eight

Even the Leaders Hurt

Many feel that the Bishop, Pastor or the church leader is this superhuman character that never goes through anything because they are so use to him or her being everything that they need but often times don't understand that even Superman was Clark Kent. If you didn't know, even the leaders hurt.

When you research statistics on church leaders walking away from churches it is alarming. Some reports say that over 1,700 pastors per month walk away from church. I say church because this number doesn't necessarily mean they walk away from God, because people often equate church and God as the same but I believe you can have a relationship with God and not necessary have to go to church.

Now to further explain that so the critics don't run with my last statement as though I have given people a license to not go to church. What I am saying is, it is the relationship with Christ that causes us to assemble together with our brothers and sister in the Lord, which really is the church, where we get the Greek word Ekklesia that means, "The Called Out Ones."

What is also staggering is the fact that 70% of pastors constantly fight depression and 50% of pastors feel so discouraged that they would leave the ministry if they could, but have no other way of making a living.

Something is radically wrong with this because my question is who motivates the motivator or who heals the one who is healing for so many others and seem like end up dying themselves. Maybe not a physical death but emotionally and psychologically leaders are crying out that they hurt too and my prayer is that we change the statistics and save some if not all of these leaders who feel they have no one to talk to or can confide in and know that it is not going to be exploited. The simple fact is even leaders hurt.

Here is another shocking statistic 70% of pastors and leaders do not have someone they consider a close friend. Wow. I guess what I am saying is that everyone needs someone even though we have God. Somebody came up with the crazy saying and that was, "All you need is God." Well, first my relationship with God is Spiritual not natural and there are something's that God is not going to be to me in the natural but will provide the relationship or the right situation that my natural needs can be met or ministered to.

Even leaders hurt because they are human too. I love this scripture from 2 Corinthians 4:7 which says, "But we have this treasure in earthen vessels, that the excellency of the power may be of God, and not of us." Another translation of that same verse says, "We have this treasure in cracked pots." The treasure is symbolic for the anointing. I see now we have the anointing in crackpots or in other words we as humans have our frailties and sometimes seem like we are all cracked up if we tell the truth.

Here is what is powerful. Although God knew we were cracked up he still placed His anointing inside of us so that we would know it wasn't us that the reliance should be placed on but most certainly it should be him and not of us. I want to speak to every Bishop, Pastor, Church leader or even parishioner and say, "It's ok to be human!" Stop allowing people to put pressure on you to be this great wonder that saves the entire world and then ends up a casualty because you bought into the hype that you were all that and a bag of chips.

I will be the first to tell people that I am not God. I am his spokesman and representative in the earth to lead people to him but trust me I didn't die on the cross for anyone. Since I didn't die for anyone the pressure is not on me to be something I never was. If we do not understand this concept, then I am afraid that we will continue to allow people to expect something from us that we can never give.

I am learning that it is ok to be human. I mean we don't have to be spiritual robots who are detached from the seat of our emotions because we have a title in front our name and a few letters behind it. Even the leaders hurt. I can say this because I too myself have been hurt. Many when they think of hurt only see or talk about how they have been hurt by pastors and church people. Has anybody even considered that the parishioners have hurt many Bishops, Pastors and church leaders?

Think about it for a minute. Everyone can walk away but the pastor has made a commitment to God to be the last man off the ship. It is like the movie the Titanic when the Captain knows very well that he had to be the last one off the ship no matter what happened. The pastor sadly to say sees people come and go and not everyone that goes is because of the church or the pastor sometimes people or just people and there nothing you can do about that. Nonetheless when you as a leader truly love souls it takes a piece of your heart when that happens. Even the leader hurts. We must if we are going to not have massive amounts of stress and anxiety on us learn how to be free from people to be free for them. If not, then whenever something happens it will rip a piece of your heart out because of the intense love that we have for God's people and people in general.

The leader often hurts silently because there aren't many people the he or she can go to where they can be totally transparent about what has brought hurt to their hearts and remember they are human too. The same things that the congregants go through the leaders go through probably ten times as much. You would think the church is the one place where you can come and be totally transparent but like I shared when I was on the national Praise The Lord program on TBN (Trinity Broadcast Network) in the movie A Few Good Men, when Jack Nicholson is on the stand being cross-examined by Tom Cruise he says, "You Can't Handle The Truth!"

Sad to say that sometimes that is the case when it comes to the church for members and leaders alike we are saying be transparent but the fact of the matter is sometimes the response is, "You Can't Handle The Truth!" So therefore, often we lead while we bleed. Pastors have committed suicide at staggering and alarming rates and only if they had some safe place to be totally open and transparent about their hurts and concerns maybe more would be with us right now.

All I am saying is even the leaders hurt. We just don't have many ears that we can speak our vulnerabilities to and not be looked at as being weak or not respected for the offices we hold. All we are saying and I guess I can be the self-appointed spokesman for all clergy now and say, "We are real people that have hearts that hurt." The bible even admonished us to pray for our leaders.

"I exhort therefore, that, first of all, supplications, prayers, intercessions, and giving of thanks, be made for all men; For kings, and for all that are in ***authority***; that we may lead a quiet and peaceable life in all godliness and honesty" (1 Timothy 2:1-2, KJV). My prayer is that if you are a pastor and reading this book that you know that my prayers are with you as a fellow colleague in the Gospel.

If you need me I am here for you. Feel free to reach out to me any pastor or church leader from around the world whether male or female because I am my brother's keeper. If you are not a pastor or church leader, then I ask that you pray for your pastor or church leader daily asking God to give them strength and the grace to do what he has called them to do. Pastoring believe it or not is a hard job because you give so much of your heart.

Yield means to slow down and stop if necessary. Pastors I must say, sometimes need to slow down and stop if necessary. Go on vacation and I mean really go on vacation. Ask God to give you an inner circle of trusted people where you can let your hair down and be real without judgment or criticism. I don't want you to stack the deck with yes men but with people that will love you enough to be a listening ear but will also be the voice of reason and correction if necessary.

I want to share this scripture from Psalms 61:2; "From the end of the earth will I cry unto thee, when my heart is overwhelmed:
lead me to the rock that is higher than I." What I am saying is that with a dedicated prayer life you can always cast all your cares on God because he cares for you. This will allow you to not overload your circuits because even the leaders hurt. I have also come to learn that meditation coupled with prayer is so powerful because it allows us to truly focus and slow our mind down and hear God.

I believe a lot of leaders hurt mentally and emotionally because we are always carrying the burdens of ministry and people around in our hearts and minds. We never let our mind rest because we are always thinking about everything and everybody except ourselves most of the time. Leaders let's slow down and smell the roses.

Let's slow down enough to notice that even the ducks at the park live carefree because their provisions come to them. Do we bring the bread and throw an entire loaf of bread right at their feet? Instead throw it to them piece by piece.

What I am saying is that we need to let go and let God. Remember leaders that the Bible tells us to cast our cares upon him for he cares for us. Have I experienced hurt as a leader? Most definitely. What has kept me going is the fact that I understand there is a balm in Gilead. The Lord is able to heal you from the inside out.

There comes a time where we have to pull from the anointing that is on the inside of us. Luke 4:23 the "a" clause of that verse says, "And he said unto them, Ye will surely say unto me this proverb, Physician, heal thyself." My prayer is that even now you will begin to cover your leader in prayer and ask God to bless the men and women of God because they have an enormous responsibility and never forget that they are real people with real feelings. If you hurt please remember even the leaders hurt.

Yield – Journal Moment

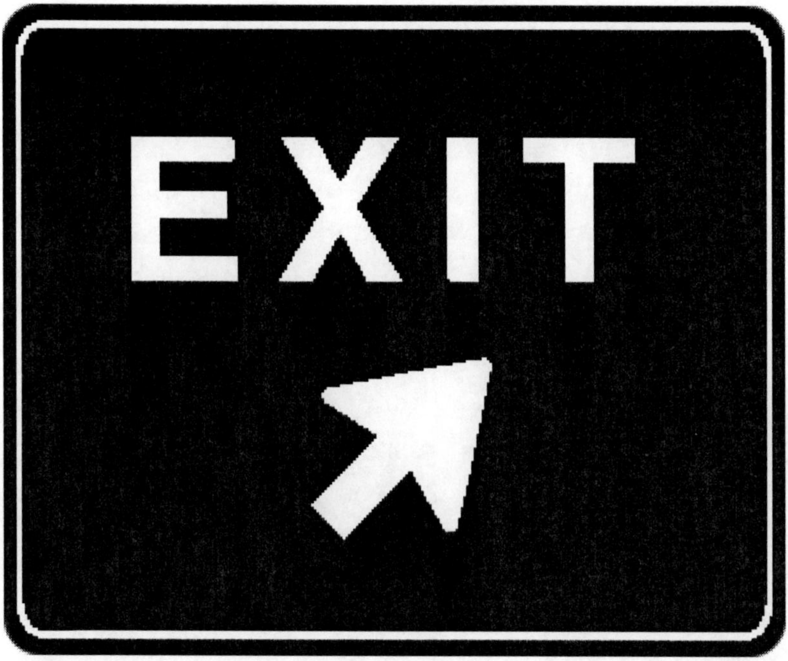
EXIT

Chapter Nine

Suffering for The Glory

"For I reckon that the sufferings of this present time are not worthy to be compared with the glory, which shall be revealed in us." This rings so true when you look at what it is really saying. The word reckon means I have added up things and have come to a conclusion. Here is my personal conclusion; whatever I have had to go through is not even worth talking about once I look at the end result of being on the other side of going through.

I use to ask God why me all the time and it is amazing how God responds to us. He response was simply this, "Why Not You?!" That got my attention so I changed the substratum of my question to a different premise and that was, "Lord what is the reason you are allowing me to go through these life issues and circumstances?" Now when I changed my attitude towards why I was going through to what was the reason then and only then did God begin to give me revelation.

It is simple no pain no gain. Sometimes our expectation is to receive something for free or as some have said, "Hook me up." Well not this time.

It is going to cost you something. The blessing in the suffering is to know that there is a great reward waiting for you on the other side of the test. Wow, there it is, testimony, the root word is test. There can never be a true testimony without going through and passing the test.

Now I will not paint a picture that it is easy going through life's challenges or that you will understand every situation in life that you must go through, but I want you to understand very clearly that God will put no more on you or I are able to handle. If you are experiencing it consider that God is trying to get something to you that he could not without allowing you to be tested, proven and tried.

Yes, we suffer but our suffering is not in vain. Our suffering has a purpose. Everything in life that we go through has a glory attached to it. I felt that! Let me say it again. Everything that we go through has a glory attached to it. The glory that is attached to what we go through does not always announce that it is there. It is often silent and then when we reach that point where we feel like we can't take anymore, that's exactly when it seems like the glory that was silent or hidden comes forth in a tremendous way.

No one likes to suffer. No one likes to experience difficult times but every time I look at the glory it does make the times of intense pressure look miniscule. As a matter of fact, let's peak at this scripture again. "And he said unto me, my grace is sufficient for thee: for my strength is made perfect in weakness. Most gladly therefore will I rather glory in my infirmities, that the power of Christ may rest upon me."

Well seems like the precursor to power is pain and suffering! I am not talking about stuff that we get ourselves into I am referring to the anointing on your life that just attracts attacks. You may be dealing with something now but trust and believe there is a glory and an anointing that is getting ready to hit your life like never before.

I want you to stay on the road and don't get off. Life is so unpredictable. Even when we think we have a plan it never goes the way we planned. The truth of the matter is you don't realize how close you are to the downpour of favor resting on your life. There is a plethora of examples where we can see individuals who stayed the course through their sufferings to reign in glory and power.

Let's take a look at a few of them. Remember Joseph who was thrown into a pit by his own brothers and then sold to the Midianites who were on their way to Egypt and we all know ultimately Potiphar's wife lies on him and he ends up in prison.

Once in prison we know he eventually interprets the dream of the butler who was supposed to remember him when he got out only to forget about him but God creates a situation to get some glory. Well you know the story he interprets the dream of the Pharaoh and implements a logistical plan that saves Egypt.

Now that's suffering for the glory to me.

Let's also take a look at Paul and Silas as they were in prison with their hands and feet locked in stocks and chains. Not even being on lock down, like that was able to keep them from praying and singing praises unto God. I feel this in my spirit. There's no way you can praise God and still remain locked up.

At midnight, they began to have devotional service (Come on somebody). The praises of God went forth and an earthquake shook. Watch this, not the whole city but where the prison was and every man's bands were loosed and every door opened.

Now that's suffering for the glory to me. What a mighty God we serve. Glory is coming to you even now because you have been going through and now it is time to walk in the glory cloud. Can I give you another revelation? The greater the suffering means the weightier the anointing and glory will be.

I hope that your mindset is beginning to change as you look at any past, present or future sufferings you may have to deal with because it always ends up for you and I to have a greater level of anointing and favor. So, the next time you hear somebody that's going through say, "Why Me?", you can lean over and tell them, "It's for the Glory!"

"For I reckon that the sufferings of this present time are not worthy to be compared with the glory, which shall be revealed in us."

Exit – Journal Moment

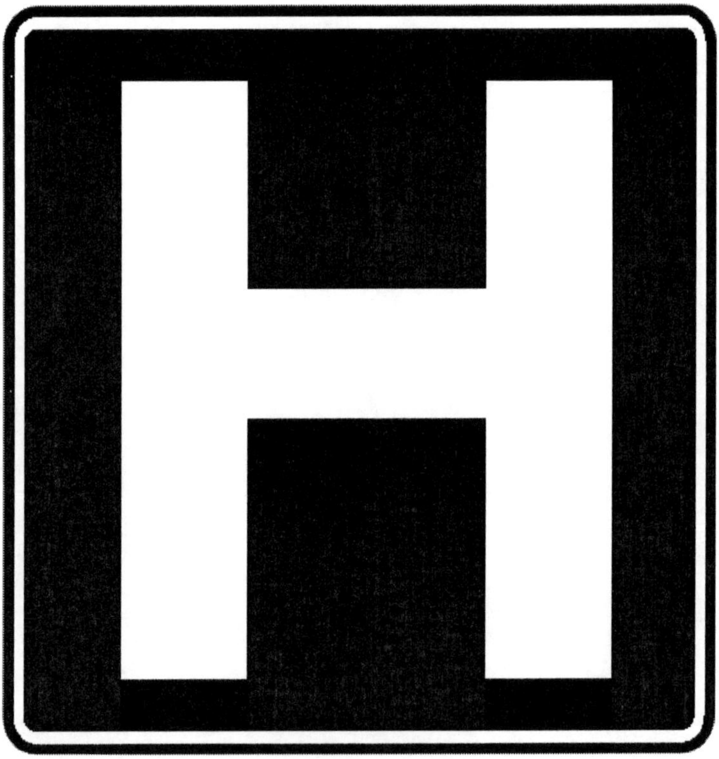
H

Chapter Ten

Healing and Restoration

It is important that we understand that in life we are going to experience things that will hurt. I don't believe that we should act like robots as though we don't feel or have emotions, after all God made us that way. I do believe that after we have gone through trying times or disappointments or even a breakup or divorce or whatever the journey that life has caused you to travel, that we take time to heal and recover. Healing and restoration is needed and necessary so that we don't take the past into our future.

Healing is something that takes time but you can make it through the healing process. One thing I constantly tell myself is don't allow what you have been through to make you bitter it should only make you better! If you and I need to be healed that must mean that something or someone has wounded us. There are wounds that are physical that you can see and then there are wounds that or emotional and psychological.

I think the latter is the most difficult to overcome but you can. When something or someone has wounded you it sometimes is a difficult thing to overcome because we don't expect those that are close to us to hurt us but unfortunately it happens. You know that old saying, "That's Life!" This time is a time where you need to seek God like never before so that bitterness does not subtly try to take root in your heart. Cry it out if you must but don't let the pain cause you to be someone who goes around beating yourself up.

I tell my brother all the time that your windshield is bigger than your rear-view mirror. What I mean by that is don't waste time looking back into your past when your future is much bigger and brighter. For some, the healing and restoration process will be different in terms of the duration of this process. A good rule of thumb is to not compare your healing process with someone else's. Everyone heals differently.

Something else that is good to have in place is a good support system. This can be your family or closest friends. You want this support system to be people that you authorize to speak into your life and not be a group of "Yes Men or Yes Women" These people should be ones that also keep you covered in prayer as you will need it.

I have come to realize in order to really heal you have to stop trying to figure out why. If you don't then you will forever be in a state that will hinder you from moving forward in your life. Some advice I gave myself in the healing and restoration process was to simply enjoy life. If you have children spend more time with them. If you love to travel, then do that. Get out and spread your wings and have a good time.

It is amazing how being on the beach somewhere helps the healing process. (I'm smiling real big right now – Ham and Cheese smile). Another thing you can try to implement into your life is meditating. Take the time to slow down and appreciate things that we normally breeze by because we are always going at 100 mph.

I want you to practice what you preach in this area because we want to help so many others get healed while forgetting about ourselves. I want you to promise that you will take some time for yourself. You deserve it!

I can remember the late Bishop Gilbert Earl Patterson saying, "Be Healed, Be Delivered and Be Set Free!" As you release and go through your healing process I want to encourage you and let you know that your best and brightest days are ahead of you.

You might be asking when will I know that the healing process is complete for me. I will say this much a clear indication will be you being able to look at what caused the hurt and pain and it not affect you at all. I mean it doesn't trigger any emotion at all negatively. You will have a pretty good idea that you are on the other side of it and truly have moved forward.

Remember this, don't short change yourself take time for healing and restoration. Time heals all wounds.

Hospital – Journal Moment

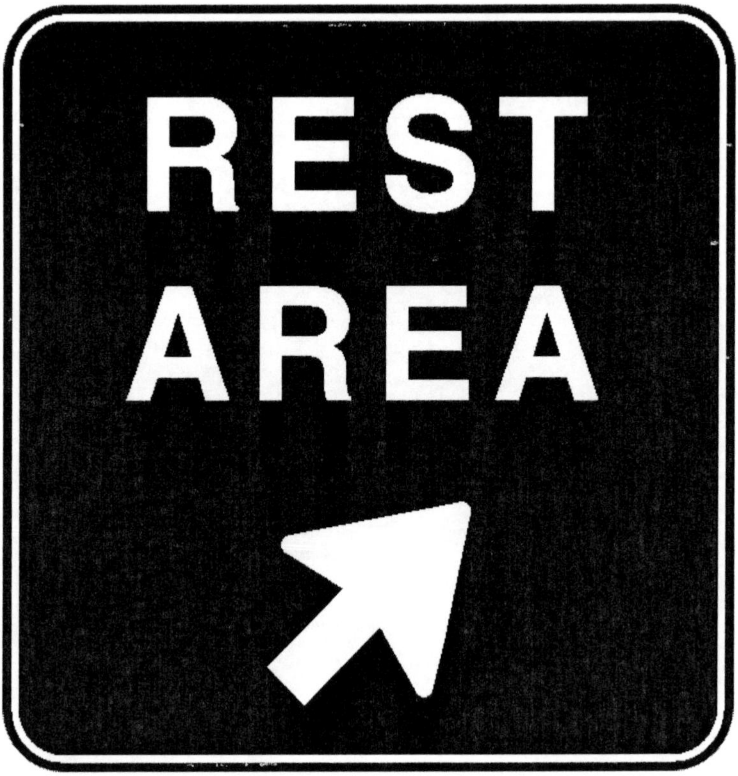
REST
AREA

Chapter Eleven

I'm Better Because of It

I have a saying that goes like this, "I'm not bitter, I'm better!" That is exactly what you have to tell yourself. Life happens and the truth of the matter is you can't beat yourself up because of stuff that most of the time we have no control over in the first place.

Quite frankly we need to stop beating ourselves up over the stuff that we did get ourselves into and realize that some kind of a way, all things truly do work together for the good to them that love God and are the called according to his purpose. Most people don't understand the power of truly moving forward and taking what you go through as a stepping-stone into your future.

Say this with me, "I'm better because of it!" Whatever your "IT" is, you are better because the "IT" pushed you to the place where you are and I am now. We spend far too much time questioning why things happen to us and not enough time celebrating that they did. I know you may be saying, "What!"

Think about it this way you wouldn't be the person you are now had it not been for what we call life. People counted you out but you're still here. They said you wouldn't accomplish anything and look at your resume. They said you wouldn't get past that divorce and look at you now.

Looks like you are better to me. Let me say it again. You are better! On every journey, there are rest areas. I like to call them an oasis along this journey called life. We all at some point need to know that there is nothing wrong with pulling over and getting off the road and taking a rest.

If you think about it the rest stops are strategically placed all along the route that you are traveling. I believe what the Lord is trying to say to us is that no matter what route we take in life, he has along the journey placed places of refreshing and rest.

When I think of being better I am reminded of a song that my good friends The Showers Family Group sings and it is entitled, "Better!" The chorus says, "Lord I want to be, I want to be better!"

Here is the question that everyone will ask. How are you better because of the things you have experienced?

All I can say is that you should take the things that you go through and learn that if it didn't destroy you it made you stronger and better. Your prayer life is better because of the things you have faced. Your service to God is better because life pushed you closer to God.

You are a winner! I had to tell you that because life will tell you otherwise. I had to tell you because I want you to always remember that you are fearfully and wonderfully made. I had to tell you because I want you to realize that the things you have gone through didn't destroy you because they couldn't.

Remember the things that you went through didn't make you bitter they only made you better!

Rest Area — Journal Moment

ABOUT THE AUTHOR

Samuel McGill III

President Barack Obama Lifetime Achievement Award Recipient, holds a Bachelor's Degree in Theology from St. Thomas Christian College and is the Presiding Bishop of All Nations Fellowship of Churches and the Establishmentarian of McGill Ministries-From Pain To Power.

Samuel McGill III is also the CEO/Program Director of Stellar Award Winning All Nations Radio and Label Executive of Seraphim Records. He is a current host of the prominent Christian Television Program "Atlanta Live" which airs in Metro Atlanta and Nationally via Direct TV and Dish Network.

Co-Host of The Christian View Television Program produced and hosted by Jackie Carpenter and is seen in approximately 78 million homes. He has made several National appearances on The Word Network, TCT Global Television and the "Praise The Lord" Program on TBN (Trinity Broadcasting Network).

Bishop McGill has appeared on the covers of Apostolic Voice Magazine, Majesty Now Magazine, Blest Magazine and Triumph Magazine. God has gifted and anointed him for this end time harvest.

He has blessed people across the U.S. and oversees with a theme message of "From Pain To Power." One thing that is consistently said about him is his love for God and people.

Bishop McGill has a deep and rich Apostolic Heritage and a heart for lost souls.

McGill Ministries, Inc.
The Worldwide Ministry of
Bishop Samuel McGill III

www.mcgillministries.org

Tune in to the best in gospel music and Christian programming 24/7 on Stellar Award Winning All Nations Radio

allnations radio

www.allnationsradio.net

www.allnationschurches.org

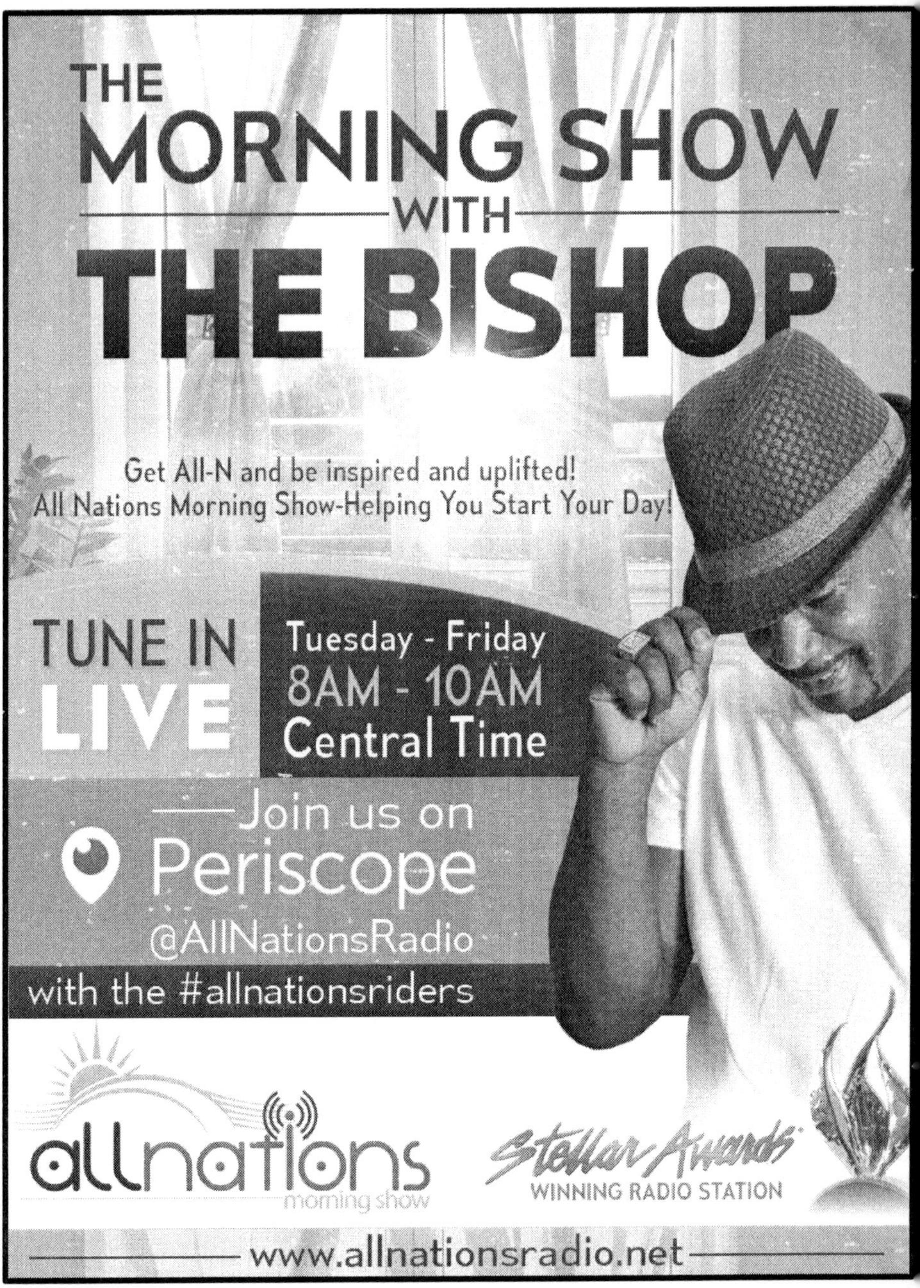
THE
MORNING SHOW
WITH
THE BISHOP
Get All-N and be inspired and uplifted!
All Nations Morning Show-Helping You Start Your Day!
TUNE IN
LIVE
Tuesday - Friday
8AM - 10AM
Central Time
Join us on
Periscope
@AllNationsRadio
with the #allnationsriders
allnations
morning show
Stellar Awards
WINNING RADIO STATION
www.allnationsradio.net

www.seraphimrecordslive.com

www.wordtherapypublishing.com

"A Message That Heals"

Tune in to our Spanish sister station with the best in Spanish gospel music and Christian programming 24/7 on Stellar Award Winning All Nations Radio

NICARAGUA allnations radio

www.allnationsradionic.net